EDGE
BOOKS

THE KIDS' GUIDE TO

Balloon Twisting

by Brad and Cindy Trusty

CAPSTONE PRESS
a capstone imprint

Edge Books are published by Capstone Press,
1710 Roe Crest Drive, North Mankato, Minnesota 56003.
www.capstonepub.com

Books published by Capstone Press are manufactured with paper
containing at least 10 percent post-consumer waste.

Library of Congress Cataloging-in-Publication Data
Trusty, Brad, and Cindy Trusty.
   The kids' guide to balloon twisting / by Brad and Cindy Trusty.
      p. cm.—(Kids' guides)
   Includes bibliographical references and index.
   Summary: "Gives kids step-by-step instructions about how to twist fun
      balloon animals and other shapes"—Provided by publisher.
   ISBN 978-1-4296-5444-9 (library binding)
   1. Balloon sculpture—Juvenile literature. 2. Balloon decorations—
      Juvenile literature. I. Trusty, Cindy. II. Title. III. Series.
   TT926.T78 2011
   745.594—dc22   2010036470

Editorial Credits
Mandy Robbins, editor; Kyle Grenz, designer; Eric Manske,
   production specialist; Marcy Morin, scheduler; Karon Dubke,
   photographer

Photo Credits
All images from Capstone Studio, except: Brad and Cindy Trusty, 32;
   Shutterstock/BonD80, 7 (marker)

Printed in the United States of America in Stevens Point, Wisconsin.
072012   006856R

Table of Contents

Have you ever been to a carnival where an entertainer was making cool twisted balloon sculptures? Believe it or not, you too can impress your friends by twisting balloons.

Balloon twisting may look like magic, but it is actually based on science. Balloons are inflated and twisted into sections. **Friction** and **pressure** hold the sections in place. Once you learn the basics, there are thousands of designs you can make.

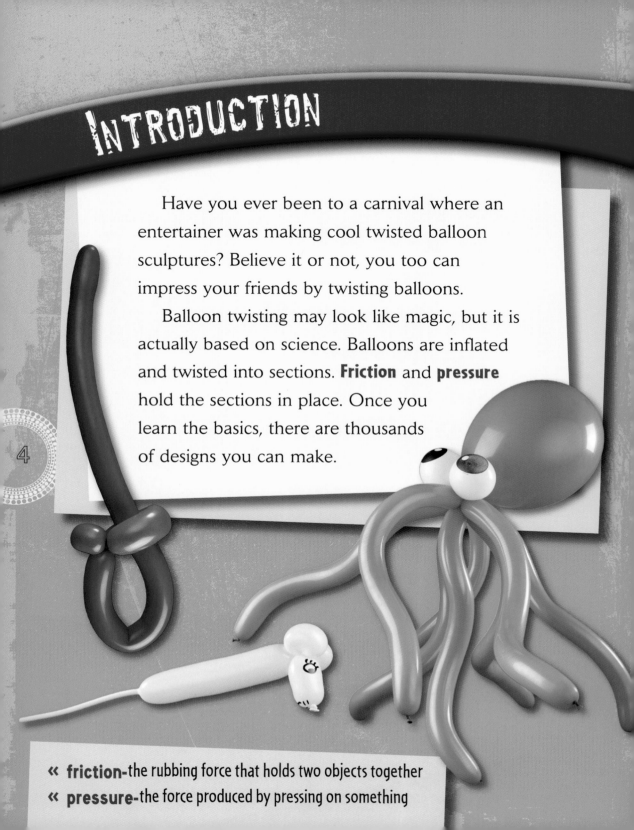

4

« **friction**-the rubbing force that holds two objects together
« **pressure**-the force produced by pressing on something

Safety First

Balloon twisting should be fun, not dangerous. Before you begin, learn a few safety rules.

1 Use a balloon pump to inflate balloons. Using your mouth to inflate lots of balloons is bad for your lungs.

2 Don't chew or bite on balloons. You could choke.

3 Keep balloons away from pets and young children so they don't choke.

What You'll Need

A "260" is a balloon that inflates to 2 inches in **diameter** and 60 inches long.

The 5-inch and 11-inch rounds are the round balloons you see at many parties.

A balloon pump is a hand-held pump that inflates balloons.

Metric Conversions	
2 in	5 cm
5 in	13 cm
11 in	28 cm
60 in	152 cm

« **diameter**-the length of a straight line through the center of a circle

I bet you didn't know you could burp a balloon! Before you begin twisting, you'll need to learn a few common balloon-twisting terms and techniques.

Inflation Size

Each balloon creation requires a specific inflation size. On a 260 balloon, size is determined by how much of a tail is left. Leaving a "3-inch tail" means you inflate the balloon until the uninflated part at the end is 3 inches long.

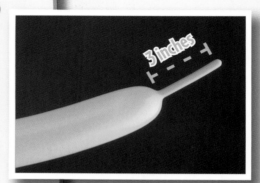

3 inches

6

Metric Conversions

3 in	8 cm

Burping Balloons

"Burping" means letting a small puff of air out of your balloon. This slightly softens the balloon and makes it easier to tie and twist. Unless you're instructed not to, you should always burp a balloon after inflating it. Tie the balloon closed, and you're ready to twist.

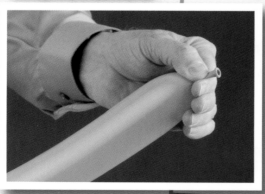

Holding Balloons

Grip balloons firmly. You need one hand on either side of the spot where the twist will appear. Gently squish the balloon with your fingers and thumbs to make it easier to twist. Then twist one hand away from you for five to eight full rotations. Doing several rotations keeps the twist secure.

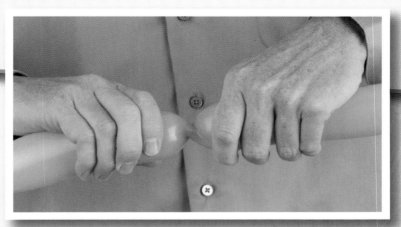

Finishing Touches

You can give your balloons extra character by drawing faces and other details with permanent markers. Drawing eyes and smiles brings your animals to life. Adding spots, stripes, and other markings makes your balloons more interesting too.

BUZZING BEE

What You Need

* one yellow 260 balloon

Let's start off with a really simple balloon—the classic bee. This is one bee that will never sting you!

1

Inflate a 260 balloon. Leave a 2-inch tail.

2

Make a 4-inch twist at the nozzle end.

3

Make a 2-inch twist at the tail end. Steps 2 and 3 form the head and body sections.

Twist the head and body sections together. This is called the **loop twist**. It will create a large loop.

Fold the middle of the loop down to where the head and body sections connect.

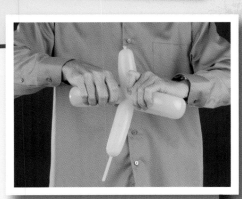

Twist the balloon into this spot.

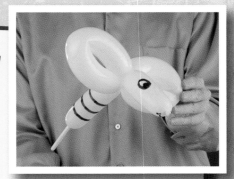

Draw eyes above the balloon's nozzle. This is the bee's face. The tail is its stinger.

9

TWISTING TIP: DRAW EYES ABOVE THE TAIL TO MAKE YOUR BEE INTO A HUMMINGBIRD.

Metric Conversions	
2 in	5 cm
4 in	10 cm

WALK THE DOG

What You Need
★ one 260 balloon of any color

Now for the classic—the balloon dog. This is the basic balloon animal shape. Once you learn this, you will be able to make a horse, giraffe, squirrel, and more!

1 Inflate a 260 balloon. Leave a 6-inch tail.

2 Starting at the nozzle end, twist a 2-inch bubble for the nose.

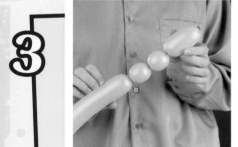

3 Keep holding the 2-inch bubble, and twist two 1.5-inch bubbles for ears. Now you have a string of three bubbles.

4 Hold the ears side-by-side and twist them together. This is called the **bubble twist**. It locks the ears in place.

Twist a 1-inch neck bubble and two 3-inch front leg bubbles.

Hold the legs together and do another bubble twist to lock them together.

Twist a 2-inch body bubble and two 2-inch leg bubbles.

Use another bubble twist to lock the leg bubbles together. The remaining balloon is the tail.

TWISTING TIP: IF IT LOOKS LIKE YOU WILL RUN OUT OF BALLOON, GIVE IT A SQUEEZE TO PUSH AIR INTO THE END.

Metric Conversions	
1 in	2.5 cm
1.5 in	4 cm
2 in	5 cm
3 in	8 cm
6 in	15 cm

Hats Off!

What You Need

* one 260 balloon of any color

To create this fun accessory, start with the basic helmet shape. You can add horns, balloon animals, and fun balloon shapes. Make your hat as crazy as you want.

1

Stretch the 260 balloon before you inflate it. This makes it long enough to make a helmet.

2 Inflate the 260 balloon, leaving a 0.5-inch tail.

3

Twist a 1-inch bubble at the nozzle end.

4 Wrap the balloon loosely around your head. Note where the balloon crosses itself.

5

Twist the 1-inch bubble around the spot where the balloon crosses itself.

Metric Conversions

0.5 in	1.5 cm
1 in	2.5 cm

6

Take the remaining tail and make a 1-inch bubble on the very end.

7

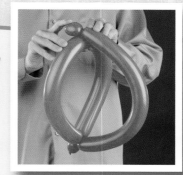

Twist this bubble into the loop across from the first 1-inch bubble.

13

8

You now have a basic helmet. Twist on any decorations you want!

THE FLYING MOUSE

What You Need

* one white, gray, or pink 260 balloon

Have you ever seen a mouse fly? You're about to! Make these balloons for your friends and see whose mouse can fly the highest.

1 Inflate a 260 balloon to 10-12 inches. This balloon will have a very long tail. Do not burp it. This will make it fly better.

2

Starting at the nozzle end, twist a 1.5-inch head bubble.

3

Hold the first bubble, and twist a 1-inch bubble to make the first ear.

4

Grab the ear bubble in the middle and pull it slightly out.

5

Twist the two ends of the ear bubble together. Steps 4 and 5 are called the **ear twist**.

Repeat steps three through five to create the second ear.

Metric Conversions

1 in	2.5 cm
1.5 in	4 cm
10 in	25 cm
12 in	30 cm

7 Draw a cute face on the first bubble to complete your mouse.

TO MAKE YOUR MOUSE FLY:

1 Make the "OK" sign with your thumb and pointer finger.

2 Rest the mouse on your hand. Dangle the tail through the loop of your thumb and finger.

4

3 Grab the tail with your other hand and stretch it back as far as you can.

Release the tail and watch your mouse soar!

Sword Fight!

What You Need

★ a 260 balloon of any color

Do you want to have a sword fight with a friend? This is a great way to do it without getting hurt. The simple sword can be made with just three twists. The knight sword requires a bit more skill.

The Simple Sword

16

1 Inflate a 260 balloon, leaving a 0.5-inch tail.

2 Twist a 1-inch bubble at the nozzle end of the balloon.

3 Next to the 1-inch bubble, twist a 4-inch bubble.

Loop Twist
see page 9

4 Loop twist the 4-inch bubble.

 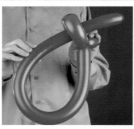 

5 Pass the front end of the balloon through the loop. Pull until you make a handle.

The Knight Sword

1 Inflate a 260, leaving a 1-inch tail.

2 Twist a 4-inch bubble at the nozzle end of the balloon.

3 Twist another 4-inch bubble, and loop twist it.

Loop Twist
see page 9

5

Ear Twist
see page 14

17

4 Make another 4-inch loop twist.

Twist two 1-inch ear twists. Place them between the loop twists.

Metric Conversions	
0.5 in	1.5 cm
1 in	2.5 cm
4 in	10 cm

SLITHERY SNAKE

What You Need

* one 260 balloon of any color
* one red 260 balloon
* Two white 5-inch rounds

This cartoony snake doesn't have scales. But it does have fun eyeballs and a long slithery tongue.

1 Inflate a 260 balloon. Leave a 0.5-inch tail.

2
Twist a 4-inch bubble at the nozzle end of the balloon.

3

Loop Twist see page 9

Pull the nozzle to the other end of the bubble and loop twist it. Wrap the nozzle around at least five times.

4
Next to the first loop, make another 4-inch loop twist.

5 Fully inflate a 5-inch white round. Burp the balloon until it is 3 inches long.

Hold the balloon in both hands with the nozzle in the middle. Twist it in half. These bubbles are your snake's eyeballs.

Twist the eyes around the spot where the mouth and body meet. This is called the **eyeball twist**. Then draw your snake's eyes.

Cut off one-third of a red 260 and inflate it. Tie the end to the inside of the snake's mouth.

19

Metric Conversions	
0.5 in	1.5 cm
3 in	8 cm
4 in	10 cm
5 in	13 cm

RAY GUN

What You Need

★ **a 260 balloon of any color**

This ray gun can be as high-tech as you want to make it. Use a permanent marker to draw switches, triggers, and power gauges.

1 Inflate a 260 balloon. Leave a 5-inch tail.

2

Starting at the nozzle end, twist a 3-inch bubble for the handle.

3

Ear Twist see page 14

Hold onto the first bubble, and do a 1-inch ear twist.

4

Twist two 5-inch bubbles.

5

Bubble twist the two 5-inch bubbles together.

6

Twist another 5-inch bubble.

7

Push this bubble between the other two 5-inch bubbles. This is called a **roll-through**. It locks the balloons together.

8

Repeat steps 4 through 7 using 2-inch bubbles.

9

Have fun drawing all the switches, triggers, and gauges you want!

21

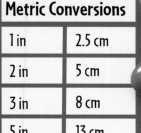

Metric Conversions	
1 in	2.5 cm
2 in	5 cm
3 in	8 cm
5 in	13 cm

TERRIFIC TENTACLES

What You Need

* a blue 11-inch round
* two white 5-inch rounds
* four blue 260s

What has 8 spindly legs, two big eyes, and an enormous head? A balloon octopus!

1 First inflate all of your balloons. Don't make any tails on your 260s.

2

Twist all four of the 260s together in the middle.

3

Tie the nozzles of the white balloons together in a knot. These will be the eyeballs.

TWISTING TIP:
IF YOU'RE TIRED OF
DRAWING EYEBALLS,
YOU CAN BUY SPECIAL
EYEBALL BALLOONS!

4

Eyeball Twist
see page 19

Eyeball twist the white balloons around where the 260s are twisted.

5

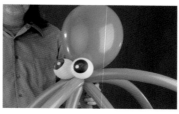

Twist the nozzle of the blue 11-inch round at the same spot where the 260s are twisted.

23

6

Twist the 260s into spirals and release them to make the tentacles curl.

Metric Conversions	
5 in	13 cm
11 in	28 cm

GONE FISHING

What You Need

* two yellow 260 balloons
* one white 5-inch round
* one yellow 11-inch round

1 Inflate two 260 balloons. Leave a 4-inch tail on each balloon.

This is one fish you don't have to keep in a bowl. Make a pole, and hook the fish for even more fun.

2

Loop Twist see page 9

Starting at the nozzle end of a 260, make a 5-inch loop twist.

3

Repeat the loop twist on the other 260. These will be the fish's lips.

4

Twist the two small loops together.

5

Inflate the 5-inch round to 3 inches. Twist it in half.

6

Eyeball Twist see page 19

Eyeball twist the white balloon onto a 260, about 4 inches back from the mouth.

7

About 4 inches back from the eyes, twist two 1.5-inch bubbles.

24

8 Bubble twist the two 1.5-inch bubbles together to make a fin.

9

Inflate the 11-inch round. Twist the nozzle around the lips. This is the fish's body.

10

Twist the 260 balloons together at the back of the fish body.

11

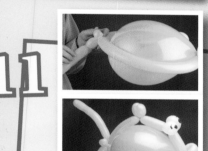

Ear Twist
see page 14

Make two ear twists to hold the tail in place. Don't forget to give your fish eyes!

Metric Conversions	
0.5 in	1.5 cm
1.5 in	4 cm
3 in	8 cm
4 in	10 cm
5 in	13 cm
11 in	28 cm

25

TO MAKE A POLE:

1 Inflate a 260 balloon, leaving a 0.5-inch tail.

2 Tie an uninflated 260 to the other balloon's tail. This is your fishing line.

3 Twist the end of the line into the fish's mouth. You just caught a fish!

ONE COOL PENGUIN

What You Need

- one white 260
- one black 260
- one orange or yellow 260

This is one penguin that is easy to keep. You don't have to keep him cool or take him fishing.

1 Inflate the black and white balloons. Leave a 1-inch tail on each.

3 Starting at the tied ends, hold both balloons next to each other and twist a 2-inch bubble.

2 Tie the nozzle ends together.

4 Twist another set of 2-inch bubbles right after the first set.

5 Twist all four bubbles together by wrapping one of the nozzle ends around the twist. Make sure the black bubbles and the white bubbles line up with each other. This will be the penguin's head.

6 Twist the black and white balloons together about 6 inches down from the head.

7

Bring the black balloon up the penguin's back. Twist it around the penguin's neck.

8

Twist another 6-inch bubble on the black 260. Bring it down and twist it onto the other three body bubbles.

9

Roll the end of the black balloon through the three black bubbles. This is your penguin's tail.

10

Now make sure your bubbles are arranged properly. The white balloons and black balloons should all line up.

11

Loop Twist
see page 9

Using the remainder of the white balloon, do two 5-inch loop twists to make the penguin's feet.

12

There should be just a small white bubble left. Hide it under the body and feet.

continue on next page

FINISHING TOUCHES

13
To make your penguin's beak, inflate the orange 260, leaving a 1-inch tail.

14

Starting from the tip of the tail, twist a bubble about 2 inches long.

15
Twist the beak bubble securely to the spot where the head and body meet. It should face out from the white eyes.

16
Cut off the remainder of the balloon with a scissors.

17
You can draw eyes, a smile, and even a bow tie on your penguin.

Metric Conversions	
1 in	2.5 cm
2 in	5 cm
5 in	13 cm
6 in	16 cm

Now that you've mastered common twists and learned some basic projects, keep twisting. You can learn to make new creations and even come up with your own. There's no end to the balloon twisting fun you can have!

29

GLOSSARY

accessory (ak-SEH-suh-ree)—something, such as a belt or jewelry, that goes with your clothes

diameter (dy-A-muh-tuhr)—the length of a straight line through the center of a circle

friction (FRIK-shuhn)—a force produced when two objects rub against each other

inflate (in-FLATE)—to make something expand by blowing or pumping air into it

nozzle (NOZ-uhl)—the open end of the balloon where air is pumped in

pressure (PRESH-ur)—a force that pushes on something

secure (si-KYOOR)—safe and well protected

Levine, Shar. *Extreme Balloon Tying: More Than 40 Over-the-Top Projects.* New York: Sterling Publishing Company, 2006.

Shores, Lori. *How to Make a Mystery Secret Smell Balloon.* Hands-On Science Fun. Mankato, Minn.: Capstone Press, 2011.

Internet Sites

FactHound offers a safe, fun way to find Internet sites related to this book. All of the sites on FactHound have been researched by our staff.

Here's all you do:

Visit *www.facthound.com*

Type in this code: 9781429654449

Super-cool stuff!

Check out projects, games and lots more at
www.capstonekids.com

ABOUT THE AUTHORS

Brad and Cindy Trusty own Cindy's Creative Celebrations, an entertainment company in St. Paul, Minnesota. They have been entertaining kids for years with amazing balloon art. Brad and Cindy hope that this book will encourage you to try your hand at this fun art form.